# Profit Not Loss

## The Story of the Baikies of Tankerness

Bryce Wilson

First published in 2003 by
Orkney Heritage

Designed and printed at
The Orcadian Limited, Hatston, Kirkwall, Orkney.

ISBN
0-9540320-5-5

Text copyright contributors separately © 2003
Illustrations copyright contributors separately © 2003

All rights reserved.
The contents of this book may not be reproduced in any form without written
permission from the publishers, except for short extracts
for quotation or review.

**The Author**
Bryce Wilson, D. A., Dip. Ed.;
Museums Officer with Orkney Islands Council (1975-2003);
Principal Teacher of Art at Stromness Academy (1971-75);
Itinerant Teacher of Art in the North Isles and Mainland of Orkney (1965-71).

Author of:
*The Lighthouses of Orkney* (Stromness Museum 1975),
*Sea Haven - Stromness in the Orkney Islands* (Orkney Press 1992),
*Arthur Dearness & The Mermaid and other Orkney Plays* (Herald Publications 2001).

Co-author of:
*No Ordinary Journey - John Rae · Arctic Explorer 1813-1893*
(National Museums of Scotland/McGill-Queen's University Press 1993),
*The Unknown Cathedral - Lesser known aspects of St Magnus Cathedral in Orkney*
(Orkney Heritage 2001).

BAIKIE OF TANKERNESS.

# Foreword

The Baikies of Tankerness were an important family in Orkney for more than three hundred years and, though they and their estate are long gone, their town house yet survives as a memorial to their days of wealth and influence. Once one of the finest residences in the Royal Burgh of Kirkwall, it is now, and has been for a generation, Orkney's principal museum.

Parts of Tankerness House date from the sixteenth century buildings which the Baikies, able and acquisitive merchant lairds, acquired (1642) and extended (1680). By the mid-eighteenth century the 6th laird of Tankerness was Provost of Kirkwall and his richly furnished home was busy with his political, business and social activities. However, the present character of the house owes most to the additions and improvements made by kelp-rich Baikies of the late eighteenth century and early nineteenth century. The 7th laird enlarged the property by buying the ancient house next to the south wing (1781). His son, the 8th laird, remodelled the north wing and added a staircase fit for the 'age of elegance'. It was a fine and hospitable place, with plenty of good music and an excellent library.

The collapse of kelp prices and the charitable bequests of the 8th laird left his successors with a diminished income. Luckily for the family these later Baikie lairds, as well as being respectable, public-spirited and popular, were quite able men who, by good management, kept their estate solvent well into the twentieth century. Then the cost of two world wars and the welfare state raised taxes so high that the doomed estate rapidly dwindled away and even Tankerness House was sold in 1951.

When lairds became obsolete and the Baikies of Tankerness left Orkney their former town house in Kirkwall, which had long been threatened by change and decay, only narrowly escaped demolition. Eventually wiser counsels prevailed and, instead of being levelled to create a car park, the building was restored for use as a museum. The growth of tourism and the development of the heritage industry have made this cultural treasure into a valuable economic asset.

The Orkney Museum, with its permanent displays and exhibition programme, has had such a great success thanks to the work of Mr Bryce Wilson and his staff. It is therefore most appropriate that one of his last tasks before retiring has been to write the story of the family that for twelve generations inhabited the building he has put to such good use.

Bryce Wilson's souvenir book *Profit Not Loss · the Story of the Baikies of Tankerness* is a worthy climax to his career as Museums Officer in Orkney. He provides us with a short, lively, well-written and beautifully illustrated account of an interesting and important family. Though intended as a popular local history his book conveys a surprising amount of information, much of it not readily available or widely-known. There is also a useful bibliography that will help Orcadians and ancestor-hunting visitors to delve into the sources of many fascinating stories. The Baikies of Tankerness are long gone but Bryce Wilson's excellent work has ensured that they will not be forgotten.

R. P. Fereday

## Acknowledgements

I would like to thank Orkney Library staff for all their assistance - Robert Leslie, Head Librarian, Alison Fraser and Phil Astley of the Archives Department, David Mackie and Colin Rendall of the Photographic Archive. I am indebted to Jean Traill Clarke, Christopher Holtom, John Windwick, Maria Pia Casarini, Lann Bain and the late Maureen Malloch for additional information on the Baikies and Cowans; the Scott Polar Research Institute of the University of Cambridge for permission to quote from the unpublished diary of Sophia Cracroft; Ray Fereday, William P. L. Thomson and Sheena Wenham for constructive comments and suggestions on the text, and Ray Fereday for kindly agreeing to write the Foreword.

## Illustrations

The photographs have been taken by Orkney Library Photographic Archivist David Mackie, or supplied from the Photographic Archive, with the following exceptions;-

Jean Traill Clarke for the photographs of her parents Robert and 'Biddy' Baikie; Margaret Walter for the wedding photograph of her parents, Grace Baikie and John Franklin; Sheena Wenham for the drawing of Captain John Baikie; Leslie Burgher for the photograph of Tankerness herring curing station.

All paintings and artefacts illustrated are held at The Orkney Museum, Tankerness House, unless otherwise indicated.

BW

Tankerness House in 1951 by D. B. Keith.

# Profit Not Loss

## The Story of the Baikies of Tankerness

*"The houses, white with harl, present crowstepped gables
and picturesque chimneys to the street . . .
through an arched gateway, one catches a cool glance
of a paven entrance court . . .
Above the doors there are inscriptions and emblems."*
Robert Louis Stevenson.

When Robert Louis Stevenson visited Kirkwall in 1869 he was impressed by the town houses of the island lairds. Among the few that have survived unaltered is Tankerness House, for more than three centuries home of the Baikies, one of Orkney's most wealthy and powerful families.

During the period of the Baikies' prosperity, wealth was based on the ownership of land. The great landowners in Orkney in the early 16th century were the Earl and the Bishop, but by the early 17th century the reformation of the Church in Scotland and the abolition of the Orkney earldom had laid open the way to wealth and power to private landowners. For the most part, influential incoming Scots were the new leaseholders and landowners, gradually ousting the long established Norse families from land and power. The Baikies, however, claimed descent from Paul Baikie, recorded by the historian Torphaeus as King Haco of Norway's sea pilot in 1263. Be that as it may, Magnus Baikie, the earliest recorded of this family, bought land in the tunship of Isbister in Birsay early in the 16th century.

The landowners or 'lairds' leased their farmland to tenants who paid their rent in kind - butter and grain, salt beef, hides, poultry and feathers and other produce of the land. Part of this was disposed of locally, the surplus then exported to Shetland, Scotland, England, Norway and other northern European countries. The rents could be sold to a middleman merchant - but greater profit was made if the lairds exported directly. Those who did so are known as 'the merchant lairds'.

To take part in foreign trade the merchant lairds from all parts of Orkney had by law to be 'freemen' or burgesses of the Royal Burgh of Kirkwall. In the mid 16th century Magnus Baikie's son Thomas was a burgess of Kirkwall. In the later 16th century his grandsons Thomas and John Baikie were prospering there, and in the 17th century his great-grandson, James Baikie (c1590-1675) became rich and powerful, a leading figure in Orkney life.

The granting of loans or 'obligements' by private individuals was at that time common practice. James Baikie at the age of 26 was already granting loans, often using the borrower's estate as security. When the borrower could not repay the loan, the land was added to Baikie's properties. In 1618 he obtained a charter of the land of Grind in St Andrews. Then in 1630 he bought land in Tankerness, and with it came the Hall of Tankerness (built in the mid-16th century for the Groat family). Baikie landholdings spread throughout the Mainland and the North Isles.

## THE ORIGIN OF TANKERNESS HOUSE

It was by means of lending money that James Baikie acquired in Kirkwall what would become 'home' for many generations of his family. The property now known as Tankerness House originated in the final flourish of the Catholic Church in Orkney, when Bishop Robert Reid built a string of church offices and manses on ground reclaimed from the Peerie Sea, opposite St Magnus Cathedral. (The medieval sea wall is buried in Broad Street. Excavations carried out in the 1970s revealed under the north wing of Tankerness House the remains of a

The arms and motto above the gateway of Tankerness House.

stone jetty surrounded by chippings of red sandstone, showing that stone for the building of the cathedral was landed there.)

After the death of Bishop Reid in 1558, all his efforts came to naught with the Reformation of the Church in 1560. Gilbert Foulzie, archdeacon and provost of St Magnus Cathedral, turned his coat and became Kirkwall's first Protestant minister. This willingness to change with the times enabled him to acquire as personal property the Archdeanery and the adjacent Sub-chantry (former home of the choir master and choir boys). Foulzie did further building on the Broad Street front, including the arched gateway surmounted by the arms of himself and his wife Elizabeth Kinnaird, and the Latin motto which means "For Country and Posterity. Unless the Lord keep them, in vain shall our seed serve him. 1574". To Foulzie is attributed the 'dole seat' - the stone platform within the courtyard on which beggars awaited alms.

Stairway tower built by Gilbert Foulzie in 1574.

## Profit Not Loss

Here the Foulzies and then their descendants lived throughout the Stewart earldom of Orkney. In the cathedral Gilbert Foulzie preached to the earl and his court. After Foulzie's death around the year 1595 the house passed to Edward Sinclair of Essonquoy (later to be Provost of Kirkwall and Member of Parliament), who had married Foulzie's daughter Ursula. From the street windows of their house this family had a grandstand view of the princely reign of Earl Patrick Stewart - 'Black Patie', grandson of King James V of Scotland - who when he stirred from the Watergate was usually accompanied by fifty musketeers and a train of gentlemen. The Sinclairs watched Eday sandstone being dragged from boats in the Peerie Sea for the building of Earl Patrick's splendid palace, 'the Newark of the Yairds', which ended with his bankruptcy and imprisonment. Then their house shook and the windows rattled when the earl of Caithness bombarded Kirkwall Castle - at the other end of Broad Street - with the king's great cannon 'Thrawn Mooth', ending the hapless rebellion of Patrick's son Robert and resulting in the execution of both.

Spiralling debts in the households of Edward Sinclair and his son Gilbert led to the sale of the house to Bishop Graham, and at length, in 1642, it came into the hands of James Baikie of Tankerness.

Far right - the Peerie Sea reaches Tankerness House garden.
Left centre - Kirkwall Castle; foreground - a 'great boat'. Wm Daniell 1820

## LIVING ABOVE THE SHOP

The position of Tankerness House on the shore of the Peerie Sea made it an ideal base for James Baikie and the generations that followed him. Here they lived above the shop. The Baikies sold estate produce, chiefly malt (sprouted and dried barley to be ground for use in brewing ale), and meal (dried oats and barley ground for bread-making), to the townspeople of Kirkwall, and exported the surplus. At that time the Peerie Sea reached the Baikies' back yard, giving direct access to distant ports.

James Baikie was also for many years factor or rent collector for the former Bishopric estates, the rents of which were now granted to the City of Edinburgh. Meanwhile he was exporting the produce of his ever increasing properties, particularly to Shetland where cash in the form of currency from Dutch fishing fleets was in good supply. And with interest on loans at 10% he became perhaps the wealthiest man in Orkney.

Every year the Baikies uplifted the rents in kind - malt, oats and bere (an ancient form of barley still grown in Orkney), butter, hides and tallow, poultry, feathers and 'wadmel' (woollen cloth) - from their properties in the North Isles (which eventually included the island of Egilsay). These joined the produce of their estates in Tankerness and other parts of the Mainland. They also traded the rents in kind purchased from other estate owners. For example, from Edward Sinclair of Essonquoy James Baikie in 1633 bought fifteen barrels of butter and a hundred meils of malt.

The boats generally owned or chartered by Orkney merchants in the 17th and 18th centuries look distinctly small for ocean voyages, but vessels of this type had been so used since medieval times. Those were the 'great boats', larger versions of the traditional Orkney yole. In 1662 *"Thomas Baikie, Skipper, in Kirkwall"* was contracted to have built for James Maxwell and John Brown in Stronsay a 'great boat' of 30 feet in the keel, planked with six strakes of oak, and with a burden of six or seven tons. Equipped with two masts and six oars she was half-decked, being an open boat apart from the covered 'foresuit' which extended to the foremast. There were also larger vessels in commission in Orkney, 'barks' or barques not exceeding 50 tons - Arthur Baikie (2nd laird) in 1678 shared ownership of *"the good shippe called the Howcare"*.

The Baikies could watch their trading vessels return from Shetland or Scotland, Norway or the Netherlands. In March 1634 James Baikie chartered *"William Flett, skipper of the bark callit the flying heart"* to carry 5000 slates from Staxigoe in Caithness to the shore in Kirkwall. At the steps of their back yard on the Peerie Sea the Baikies supervised the landing of wool, timber, tar and iron, wines and spirits. They brought home in small quantities the luxuries which leavened the lives of the landed families in their remote and windswept island homes. The Grahams of Breckness in 1664 were supplied with gloves, paper, tobacco, golf clubs and golf balls, sealing wax, ribbons, nails, white sugar, vinegar and beer glasses. In the same year William Young, receiver of the earldom rents, was billed for tableware and materials for the repair of furniture, upholstery, carpets and hangings, while in 1669 James Wallace, then minister of Lady Parish, Sanday, but later of St Magnus Cathedral, owed £16 scots for pots and pans, plates, spoons, candles and oil-lamps. More than a century later, Robert Baikie's account with Mrs Moir in Edinburgh, whether for himself or his customers, included *"3 3/4 yards Superfine blue Cloath...2 pair ribd. black silk hose...1 Superfine beaver Hatt...1 Gold Cord & Tassel..."*.

Tankerness House was one of the largest of the many houses in Kirkwall used by the island lairds for business and pleasure; the latter particularly during the winter when they brought their families to town to enjoy the company of their social equals.

It is recorded that no 'gentlemen' were resident in Tankerness, St Andrews Parish, in the late 18th century, and indeed it appears that the Baikies made their Kirkwall dwelling their year round home and business quarters, within easy reach of their principal estate.

The west wing of Tankerness House, built in 1680. *G. W. Wilson.*

James Baikie the 3rd laird continued the process of expanding the house begun by Gilbert Foulzie a century before. In 1680 he built the west wing, joining the former Archdeanery to the Sub-chantry and forming the courtyard which we see today. In the process part of an inscription in red sandstone on the wall of the Sub-chantry was obscured, but we can still read the words "...HEIR BE GOD". Despite the family's money problems at that time, the putt-stone of the south wing shows that it was extended in 1722 by Robert Baikie the 5th laird, who ran the estate on behalf of his ailing father George.

The ground floor of Tankerness House was a service area, taken up with wash house, laundry and peat house, along with kitchen, larder, dairy, brew house, cellars for wine and ale, and servants' quarters. Great ingleneuk kitchen fireplaces must have existed in both the north and south wings when they were separate buildings - two still exist in the south wing, the former Archdeanery. There would have been stores for merchandise, and a 'booth' or shop on Broad Street.

Inscribed lintel of the Sub-chantry.

1722 putt-stone of the south wing.

Ingleneuk fireplace of the former Archdeanery.

*Profit Not Loss*

Steps up to the balcony of Tankerness House.

The first floor and attics were reserved for the family and their guests. There were no passages and each room opened into the next. The public rooms were finely wood panelled. The balcony over the courtyard gate gave a detached view of street activity, as did the small panelled parlour in the north wing overlooking Broad Street. (Here claret may have been spilled when gunshots a few yards away announced the fatal wounding of Captain Moodie of Melsetter, who was attacked by James Steuart of Burray and his men on 26th October 1725 O.S.)

Tankerness House contained all the comforts available to a family of means. When James Baikie the 6th laird died in 1764 his wife Janet Douglas listed its contents, leaving a vivid impression of the hospitality of the period. In the *"Dining Roome"* there were tables of walnut and mahogany, twelve leather bottomed chairs and two elbow chairs, services of silver and pewter, delftware and stoneware.

Baikie family silver.

Mantle clock, Tankerness House.

There were hundreds of linen napkins and *"fifty Table Cloathes, large and Small"*; gilded mirrors and brass candlesticks. In other apartments were a clock, writing desks and easy chairs, feather beds, sheets and blankets. In the brew house were knocking stone and mallet, brewing kettle, masking shovels and *"Three Fats* [vats] *Small and Great"*, while the *"Bigg* [beremeal] *Cellar"* contained ten gross wine bottles and fourteen ale casks. Other 'cellars' on the ground floor held meal girnels and butter-making equipment, for which the byre in the yard accommodated three milking cows and four calves. Much of the yard was a kitchen garden, as home produced vegetables were an essential part of the diet. The myriad contents of the kitchen included *"six speets* [spits] *Small & Great...a Brass frying pann & one Iron Do. ...one large Tea Kettle...Two Copper Coffee potts...Two pewther basons... one Iron Flesh Fork...Twelve Wooden plates, Small & Great, one Yettling Pann...and One Oven."*

Until the 19th century and the advent of steam-powered shipping, travel to and from Orkney depended on wind and tide and was often hazardous through bad weather or piracy. Those who had business to attend to in Edinburgh were advised to make their Will before setting out. Arthur Baikie the 2nd laird died during a visit to Edinburgh and was buried there in Greyfriar's Kirkyard. He served as Provost of Kirkwall, 1674-79, at a time when there were more than eighty registered freemen in the burgh. In addition to the regulation of trade and the annual markets, the council of magistrates dealt with

Vinaigrette and smelling bottle.

infringements of burgh law. When William Buchanane was taken to task for building a stack of peats in the street, he *"defamed and abused"* Arthur Baikie, *"calling him ane theiff and ane knave"*, laying *"hands upon him, thursting and thumping him on the breast, seall. Times wt. His hands, in pres. of the Magistrats."*

Arthur Baikie has been described as *"one of the ablest public men that has ever taken part in the municipal government of Kirkwall"*. However, when private interests clashed with public duties, personal advantage came first. When Kirkwall Town Council petitioned to be granted the duties on liquors consumed in the town to be spent in the town 'for the common good', Provost Baikie was sent to Edinburgh at public expense to plead their cause. This he did to good effect, and was presented with a signed licence containing blank spaces to be filled in by the council. It is recorded that he then *"did, in a baise and unhandsome manner, fill up his own name yrin"*, and proceeded to pursue his fellow merchants for the liquor duties on his own behalf.

Despite the success in business of the 1st laird James and his son Arthur, trouble was just around the corner. When Arthur's son James the 3rd laird died young in the year 1700, Arthur's younger brother George succeeded him. George spent a year imprisoned in the Tolbooth of Kirkwall for debt. The Magistrates had to write to his son Robert *"to see what course he would fall upon for payment of George Baikie, his father, his tolbuith mealls in regard his said father has been near a year in prison and no part of his tolbuith mealls paid..."*.

George's son Robert's youthful exploits illustrate the lawless behaviour of the period that caused the citizens of Kirkwall to bar their courtyard doors at night. On 3rd July 1702 he and two companions attacked James Fea in *"ane mad and furious manner, with drawn swords, staves and stones to the effusion of his blood in large and great quantities"*. For this Tankerness was fined £50 scots, with an additional £6 to defray Fea's medical expenses.

The following year Robert fell afighting with his near neighbour in Kirkwall James Graham of Grahameshall, *"each of them with Kains in their hands...Beat, Bloode, bruise, and abuse one of them with the other..."*. They were each fined £10 scots, but Robert's subsequent reference to Graham as *"villane, knave, and raskall"* ensured the further penalty of £50 scots for defamation of character.

In February 1707 Robert acted as second to Andrew Young of Castleyards when he fought an unlawful duel with the merchant Hugh Clouston on the Ba' Lea of Kirkwall. When that same year Robert challenged John Traill of Elsness to a duel, the magistrates placed them under house guard. Both escaped. *"Baikie...drew his sword and pursued the whole guard, sending them about their business"*. He then attacked the burgh treasurer with his sword *"in face of severall Magistrates"*, wounding him in the hand and face. He and Traill were locked in the Tolbooth, and after trial were fined - Baikie £1000 scots, Traill 500 scots merks. The duel was abandoned.

Robert as 5th laird did nothing to reduce the debts on the estate, which at his death amounted to 50,000 scots merks. It was only after his death in 1724 that a group of shrewd and experienced trustees restored the estate to solvency on behalf of his young son James, 6th of Tankerness. In 1753 James Baikie's lands were worth £1000 and more a year.

After the Union of the Parliaments in 1707 new import duties had been imposed in Scotland. Smuggling now became commonplace among the merchant lairds of Orkney. From ports such as Rotterdam, brandy and gin, tea, spices and tobacco were brought in secretly under the noses, if not with the collusion, of the excisemen. James Baikie along with other freemen of the Royal Burgh of Kirkwall signed an agreement to discourage smuggling: *"after the 10th April 1733 we shall not drink any of the said spirits in any public house, and shall endeavour to detect and discover the Importer or retailer of such spirits"*. Again in 1744 they resolved *"to do their endeavour to put down the practice of smuggling"*. Despite these virtuous gestures, smuggling only died out in the 19th century when duties were lowered.

James Baikie as Provost of Kirkwall (1737-64) and Andrew Ross, chamberlain of the earldom estate for Lord Morton, and Sheriff-depute, were the two most important men in Orkney in the mid-18th century. They managed local elections in the interest of the Earl of Morton who was a strong supporter of the House of Hanover, and both had to flee to Shetland when in early April 1746 Orkney was briefly invaded by Jacobite Highlanders.

Lairds' incomes were never better than in the 18th century. When a string of European wars prevented the import of Spanish barilla and other sources of alkali for Britain's growing glass and soap industries, the best British source - kelp, the ash of burnt seaweed - came into its own. Orkney with seaweed in abundance became Britain's main supplier and modest estate incomes grew out of all proportion. In the late 18th century Robert Baikie the 7th laird made a thirty year lease of farm land to a tenant in Eday at an annual rental of 30-35 tons of kelp. The cottage industry of the manufacture and export of linen and linen yarn also took root and flourished in the islands.

Robert Baikie, described as *"a polite, well informed, hospitable country gentleman"*, used some of the proceeds of lucrative kelp shores to amass a wide ranging library of which some 500 volumes survive. They comprise contemporary poetry, drama and novels, books on history, science and geography, dictionaries and grammars, including the works of Swift, Congreve, Fielding, and Johnston. They have remained in Tankerness House, giving a unique glimpse of the literary tastes of a wealthy provincial Scots family two centuries ago.

Robert Baikie, 7th of Tankerness.

Books from Robert Baikie's library.

Robert Baikie was five times Master Mason of Lodge Kirkwall Kilwinning. Among his activities in a period of Masonic idealism (symbolized by Mozart's opera The Magic Flute) he founded the town's first "string band" or orchestra - an involvement in musical performance which would be continued by later generations of the family.

Elected MP for Orkney in 1780, Robert Baikie was immediately unseated for alleged irregularities during the election. He then engineered the appointment of the notorious smuggler George Eunson as customs officer with instructions to expose his political opponents as smugglers, while turning a blind eye to the smuggling activities of Robert and his friends.

In 1781 Robert Baikie bought the Chancellory which bordered Tankerness Lane, completing the property that we know today. His marriage to Mary Balfour (great-great-granddaughter of Murdoch Mackenzie the last Church of Scotland Bishop of Orkney) on 13th February 1785, was announced in the London Chronicle a month later.

The south wing, the former Archdeanery.

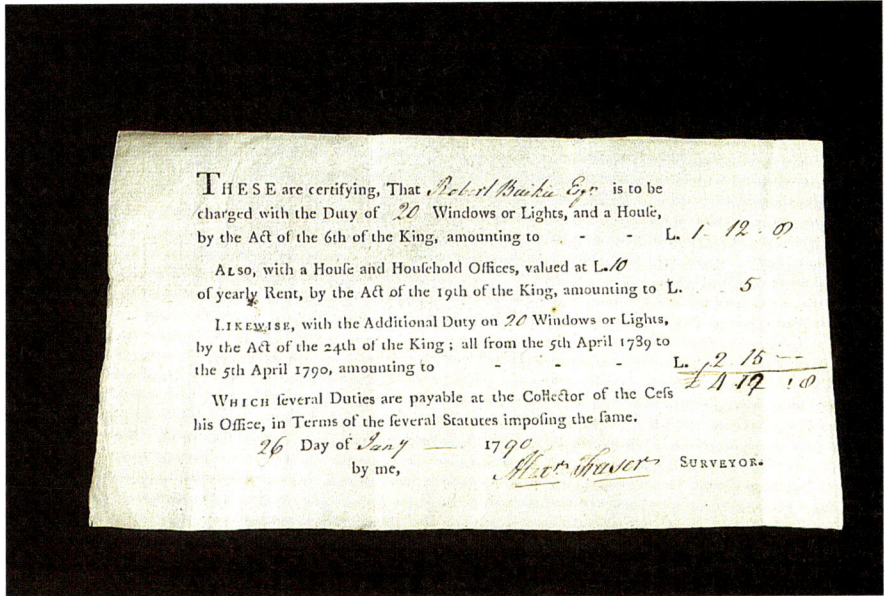

Window Tax demand for Tankerness House.

Along with other lairds Robert Baikie, a man of no military experience, was, as a reward for political favours, awarded a captaincy of the newly formed Orkney and Shetland Fencibles in 1793. The following year he took his turn in commanding the company at Fort Charlotte in Lerwick (the Fencibles were disbanded on Christmas Day, 1797).

On a visit to Orkney in 1814 Sir Walter Scott recorded in his diary: *"we dine at the inn and drink the Prince Regent's health...Mr Baikie of Tankerness dines with us."* Robert Baikie told Scott of recently deceased inhabitants of the island of North Ronaldsay who recited in the old Orkney Norn tongue the poem 'The Fatal Sisters'. Robert died in 1817.

The sons of Robert Baikie were not immune to the 18th century high living which in the early years of the 19th century still typified and sometimes ruined the lives of 'young men about town'. William Baikie returned from naval service to a life of dissipation and died diseased and penniless in London.

E for 1785.   March 12—15.

forth amongſt the trading intereſt of the whole weſtern coaſt of this kingdom, and the moſt ſtrenuous efforts are preparing to counteract a ſcheme, calculated to procure ſuch trifling, partial, and local advantages, whilſt it is ſo evidently prejudicial to commerce in general.

On the 13th ult. was married at Kirkwall, in Orkney, Robert Baikie, Eſq; of Tankerneſs, to Miſs Mary Balfour, ſecond daughter of Mr. Thomas Balfour, Merchant in Kirkwall.

STOCKS *this Day at One o'Clock.*

| | |
|---|---|
| Bank Stock ſhut | 3 per C. Old Ann. ſhut |
| 4 per C. An. 1777, ſhut | Do. New Ann. 54 ½ a ⅝ |
| 3 per Cent. conſ. 55 ¼ a ¼ a ⅜ | Do. 1751, — |
| | Ind. Stock, ſhut |
| 3 per Cent. red. ſhut | 3 per Cent. An. — |
| 3 per Cent. 1726, — | India Bonds, paid — |
| Long Ann. 16 13-16ths a ⅞ | Do. unpaid, 3s. Dif. |
| | Navy Bills, 15 per C. |
| —— Ann. 1777, — | Dif. |
| Do. 1778, — | 3 per Cent. Subſc. — |
| Navy 5 per Cent. 88 ⅛ a ¼ a 88 | Omnium, — |
| | Excheq. Bills, — |
| South Sea Stock, — | Prizes, — |

## CHAMBER of MANUFACTURERS of GREAT BRITAIN.

MR. SMEATHMAN (the Secretary) will attend every day, from Ten in the morning till Three in the afternoon, at the George and Vulture Tavern, Cornhill.

And the Committee of the above Chamber, will, during the time the treaty with Ireland is pending in Parliament, ſit from Eleven to One; when they will be glad to receive from or communicate to the Manufacturers of this City

London Chronicle, March 1785, announcing the marriage of Robert Baikie and Mary Balfour.

*Profit Not Loss* 29

His brother James, the eldest son, studied law in Edinburgh and had a reputation for high living. After he succeeded his father in 1817 he was obliged to borrow £1000 from the Kirkwall merchant James Spence. He increased the debt to £5000 in 1822, when the Commercial Bank of Scotland took a bond over the Tankerness estate. This was a dangerous period which, with kelp prices in serious decline, would have spelt the end of the Baikie estate. The day was saved when, in 1824, Samuel Laing of Papdale, who owned half of the island of Eday, bought James Baikie's half of the island. James now cleared his debts. His brother William's sad demise along with the evangelism of the period no doubt encouraged James to exchange excess for religion and to concentrate on the good management of his estates.

James Baikie, 8th of Tankerness.

With the end of the kelp and linen trade after the Napoleonic wars, Orkney lairds were forced to find other means to sustain their incomes, and turned their attention to their long neglected farmlands. With the advent of a steamship service, subsistence farming based on the growing and export of grain was replaced by the rearing and export of live cattle. Farming prospered and there was every incentive for agricultural improvements. His new found wealth allowed James Baikie to finance the improvement of farming in his Tankerness lands. He also invested in fishing - the herring curing station which he built near the Hall of Tankerness was in operation from 1833.

During the 19th century the revolution in farming meant that estate rents gradually ceased to be paid in kind and the lairds withdrew from trade. Some pursued careers in the army, navy and empire, but James Baikie was a resident landlord.

James Baikie's herring curing station in Tankerness. *L. Burgher.*

*Profit Not Loss*

The north wing of Tankerness House, remodelled in 1820. *T. Kent.*

The 1820 staircase of Tankerness house.

Marquetry long case clock, early 18th century.

In 1820 he remodelled the north wing of Tankerness House (the former Sub-chantry) in the style of the New Town of Edinburgh (except for the Broad Street extension with its spiral stone staircase, built by Gilbert Foulzie in 1574). The courtyard door opened now onto an elegant curved stairway leading to a spacious drawing room, a large dining room, and bedrooms above. Instead of panelling, the walls in the new rooms were plastered and papered, and the plaster of the stairway walls was scored to resemble blocks of freestone. The old dining room of the south wing (the luxurious contents of which were described by Janet Douglas in 1764), was enlarged by the removal of a partition to become library and smoking room. The extensions of 1820 included a large kitchen with range and ovens adjoining the north wing, along with mews containing stable and coach house and 'booths' for letting to visiting merchants at the Lammas Fair.

A close friend of the leading Secession Church minister and evangelist Dr Robert Paterson, James was bountiful in his contributions to charity (later generations took the rather rueful view that this erosion of the family fortune amounted to 'fire insurance'!).

*Profit Not Loss* 33

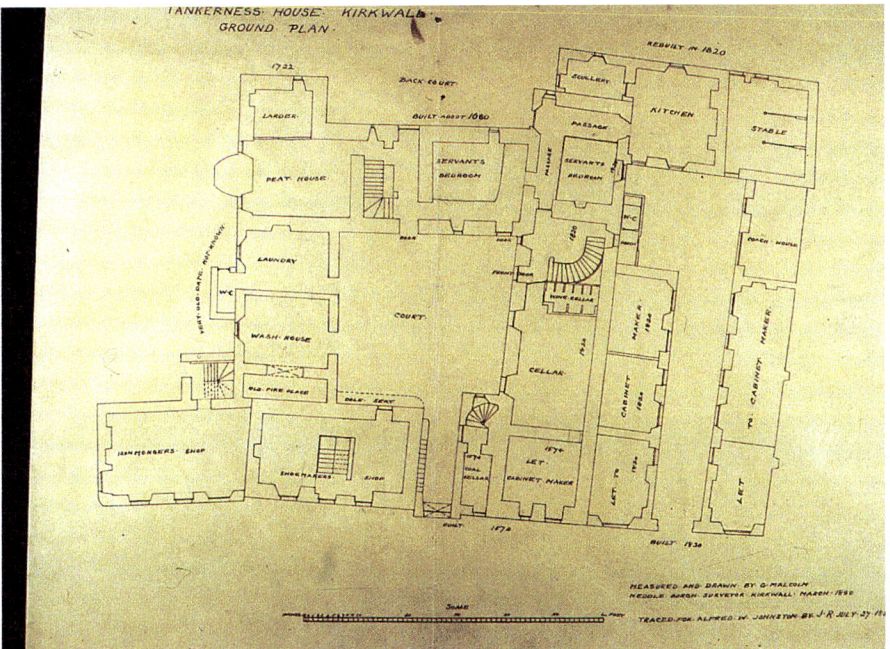
Ground floor plan of Tankerness House in 1890.

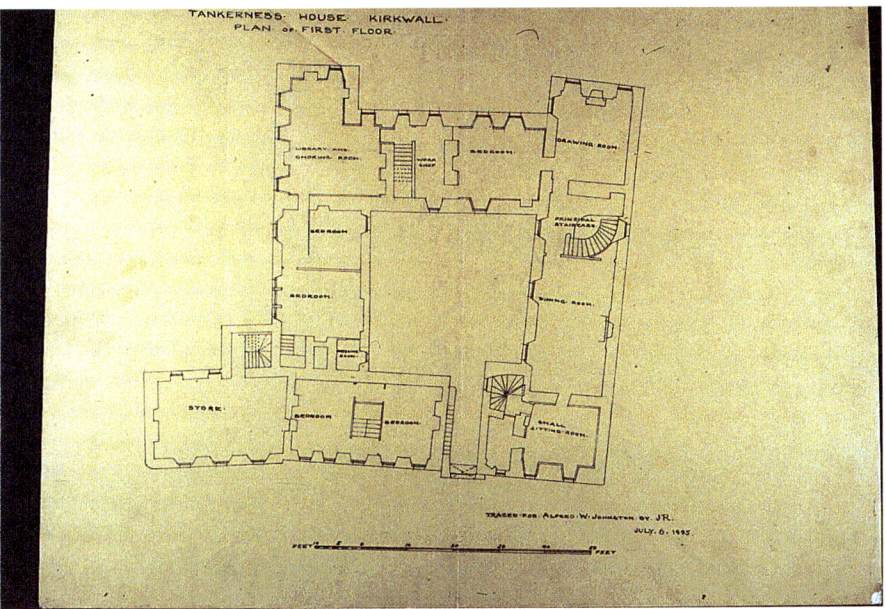
First floor plan of Tankerness House in 1890.

James Baikie, 8th of Tankerness.

In 1845 Dr Paterson officiated at the launching and naming in Kirkwall of James Baikie's gift to the Old Calabar Mission - a sloop called *The Friend of Africa*, valued at *"three or four hundred pounds"*. He donated to the United Presbyterian Church Mission Board the substantial sum of £1000 to form a scholarship for student missionaries. James Baikie served as Provost of Kirkwall 1836-1850, and was in 1854 appointed Vice-lieutenant of Orkney and Shetland.

Following the 19th century fashion for country living James and his wife, Eleanor Wemyss of Cuttlehill in Fife, had begun to spend their summers at the Hall of Tankerness. They planted trees; plane-tree, fir, ash and willow, and extended the 16th century house. Lady Jane Franklin, in Orkney seeking news of her husband's lost Arctic expedition in August 1849, visited with her niece Sophia Cracroft, who recorded in her diary: *"The former back of the dwelling (looking to seaward) has been converted into the front, by the addition of an <u>iron</u> diningroom of very handsome proportions which projects from the main building, and came down ready made and needing but a few hours to put it up...A lofty verandah supported by light pillars runs along one side and the end, and is connected with a greenhouse which runs round a large portion of the house, a very rational and delightful addition to any house in these latitudes...."*

James Baikie's 'iron diningroom' and greenhouses at the Hall of Tankerness.

Greenhouse at the Hall of Tankerness.

In 1869, at the age of 83, James Baikie died at the Hall of Tankerness after a fall from his horse. He was succeeded in the estate by his brother Robert as 9th laird.

Dr Robert Baikie M.D. had studied medicine at Edinburgh University and joined the East India Company as an assistant surgeon. While in India he took up medical research, publishing *Observations on the Neilgherries* (a treatise on climate and its effect on health). He also became an authority on native languages and translated the works of native authors. A manuscript copy of his unpublished *Journal of an Overland Journey from England to India, 1828* is lodged with the Orkney Library Archives.

Dr Baikie returned during James's lifetime to live in Kirkwall. He built Buttquoy House and founded a branch of the Scotch Metereological Society, but it is recorded that *'the climate did not agree with him'*. He and his wife Helen Davidson went to live in Edinburgh. He continued for some years to practise medicine at 55 Melville Street where, according to his obituary, *'His poor, non-paying patients, as well as those who could afford a generous fee, were alike received with the same unvarying courtesy and attention'*.

Buttquoy House, Kirkwall.

On succeeding to the Tankerness estate in 1869 Dr Baikie cancelled the arrears of the tenants, eventually entrusting the running of the estate to his grand-nephew William Dover Cowan. Despite his absence from Orkney he succeeded his brother as vice-lieutenant of Orkney and Shetland. On his death in 1889 in his 90th year he was buried according to his wishes beside his late wife in St Magnus Kirk on the island of Egilsay, which was part of the Baikie estate.

Robert and Helen Baikie had no children, so the inheritance of the estate now lay with William Dover Cowan, elder son of Robert's niece Deborah.

Deborah H. Dover, daughter of Robert Baikie's sister Mary, had married her second cousin William Cowan, who was born and brought up in Kirkwall before pursuing a career as a stock broker in London. The family returned to Kirkwall around 1860. At a time when most family entertainment was home produced, the Cowan children were enthusiastic writers and performers.

Mary Baikie or Dover, by Henry Tidey.

Profit Not Loss                                                                 39

Captain Joseph Dover, husband of Mary Baikie.

Malcolm Cowan, later Captain Malcolm Cowan R.N., father of William Layman Cowan.

With cousins and friends in the 1860s they wrote plays, poems and stories. They had playbills printed and held readings and plays in the dining room of *"Grand Uncle James Baikie"* at Tankerness House (the adjoining small parlour was christened *"The Green Room"*). Performances may also have been held in the barn loft at the Hall of Tankerness. The collected manuscripts of the group, over a hundred works known as *The Minervian Library,* of which only about half have survived, were intended as a lending library for friends in Kirkwall.

# DRAMATIC PROGRAMME

To Commence at 7·30, with the
TRAGICAL, COMICAL, DEMONIACAL, AND WHATEVER-YOU-LIKE-TO-CALL IT

## BURLESQUE
OF
## ALONZO THE BRAVE,
OR
## Faust and the Fair Imogene.

### CHARACTERS.

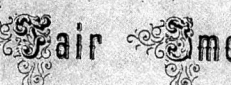

| | | |
|---|---|---|
| ALONZO, | (Pupil to Faust, a Captain in the Dirty First Volunteer Rifle Corps) | Miss BREMNER. |
| DR. FAUST, | (X.Y.Z.A.B.C.—Professor in Muddleberg College), | MR. J. A. BRUCE. |
| MEPHISTOPHELES, | (A Character, without one), | MR. SPENCE. |
| SYBIL, | (A simple Girl, the *currant* of whose thoughts flows in the direction of Jam), | Miss M. COWAN. |
| PIPO DE CLAYO, | (Sergeant in Alonzo's Company), | DR. SPENCE. |
| IMOGENE, | ("The Fair," *PAR EXCELLENCE*, now that the Lammas Fair at Kirkwall is past), | MISS C. COWAN. |
| DAME MARTHA, | (Imogene's Nurse and Guardian), | Miss A. BAIN. |

SCENE I.
**Faust's Study.**
The Opening Chorus—"HAND OH! HAND OH!"—
*Composed expressly for this occasion
by Ever<sup>d</sup> B. Holmes.*

SCENE II.
ROOM IN IMOGENE'S HOUSE.

SCENE III.
EXTERIOR OF IMOGENE'S HOUSE.

SCENE IV.
DITTO.

SCENE V.
IMOGENE'S HOUSE.

AN INTERVAL OF HALF AN HOUR.

TO BE CONCLUDED WITH

## THE LAUGHABLE FARCE
OF
## THE AREA BELLE,

### CHARACTERS.

| | | |
|---|---|---|
| PITCHER, | (In the Police), | MR. SPENCE. |
| TOSSER, | (In the Guards), | MR. FRASER-ROBB. |
| WALKER CHALKS, | (A Milkman), | MR. J. A. BRUCE. |
| MRS. CROAKER, | ("The Missus"), | MR. EVER<sup>d</sup> B. HOLMES. |
| PENELOPE, | (The Area Belle), | MISS COWAN. |

SCENE—A KITCHEN.

## GOD SAVE THE QUEEN.

Programme of a performance at Tankerness House.

*Profit Not Loss* 41

After the death of James Baikie the Cowans lived in Tankerness House. Here William pursued his interests as an amateur naturalist. Great-grandson of the 6th laird, and of a Parisian optical instrument maker, he built his own microscope, grinding the lenses himself. William Cowan's grand-daughter Margaret records: *"His greatest interest was making slides of sea, loch, burn, ditch, bog. (And the Town water supply, which caused him alarm and pessimism!)...In the course of his studies he discovered an unknown organism which turned out to be the cause of phosphorescence in summer seas. It was accepted by the Royal Society, and called 'Nocti Luca'...were it not for inherited skills, Grandpappa would not have made the microscope. It was a mixed blessing, because he would make slides of all we had eaten at lunch parties, and then show them to everyone after the meal was eaten!"* William Cowan died in 1916 at the age of 93.

Deborah H. Dover or Cowan by Henry Tidey, 1859.

William Layman Cowan, husband of Deborah Dover, by Henry Tidey, 1859.

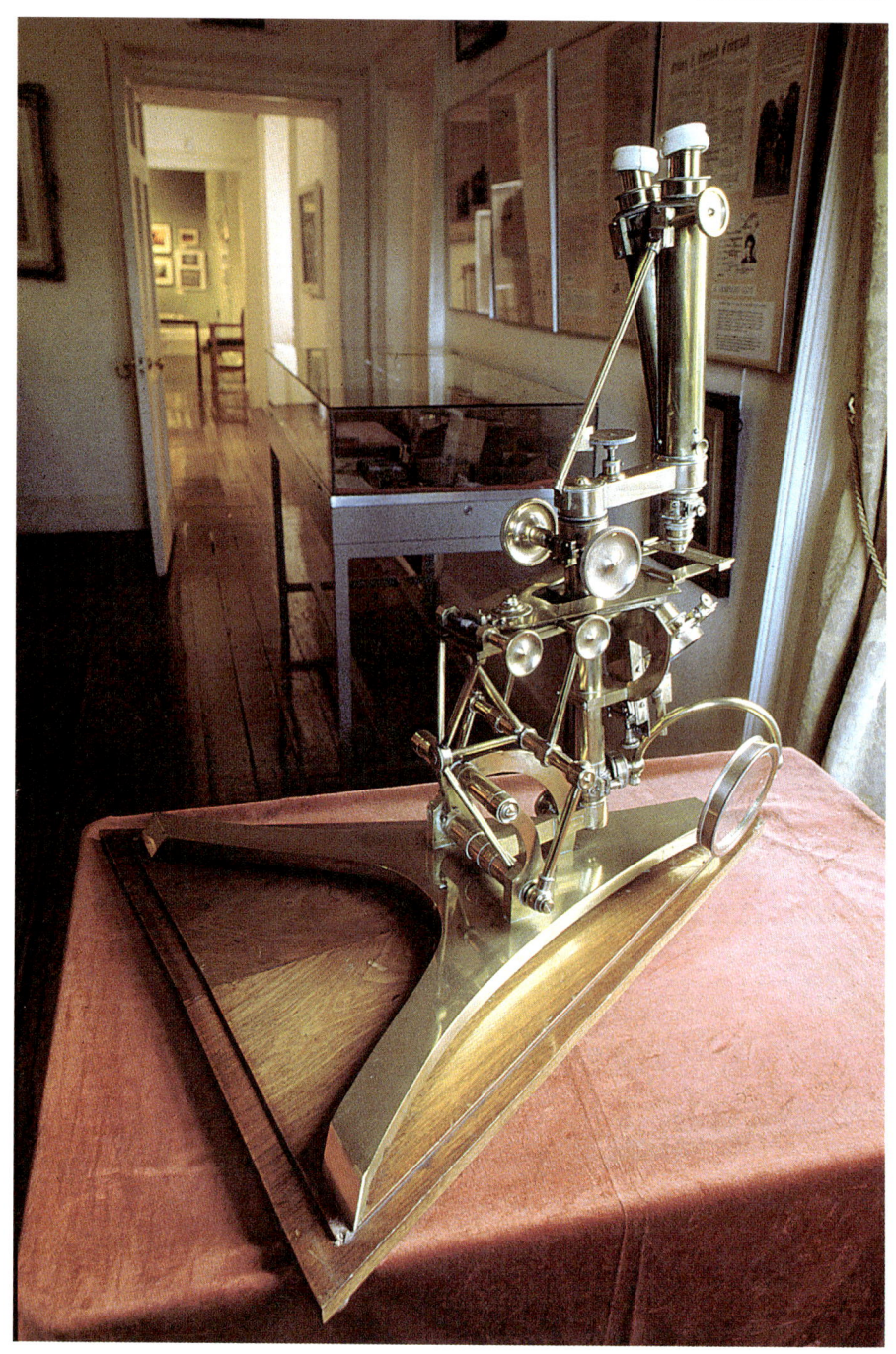

Microscope built by William Layman Cowan.

William Dover Baikie, 10th of Tankerness.

His son William Dover Cowan, having changed his name to Baikie as a condition of succession, became 10th laird in 1889. 'Dover Baikie', as he was known, is recorded as having rebuilt the homes of many of his tenants and taken a large part in local affairs, serving as a county councillor and sitting on various boards and committees. He was remembered as *"a brilliant billiards player"* and *"probably the finest shot in the north"*. An accomplished violinist, he served as president and conductor of the Volunteer Amateur Orchestral Society of Kirkwall. His wife, Johanna D. Fotheringhame of Lynnfield, published in 1894 a book of tales for children, 'Queen of the Caves', inspired by Orkney history and folklore.

Johanna Fotheringhame, wife of William Dover Baikie.

Late in the 19th century the booths in the mews of Tankerness House were let to a cabinet-maker. The Broad Street shops were now let to a shoemaker and an ironmonger. Tenants including a builder and a farrier rented the byre and stables in the yard at the back of the house.

Tankerness House in the late 19th century. *J. Valentine.*

*Profit Not Loss* 45

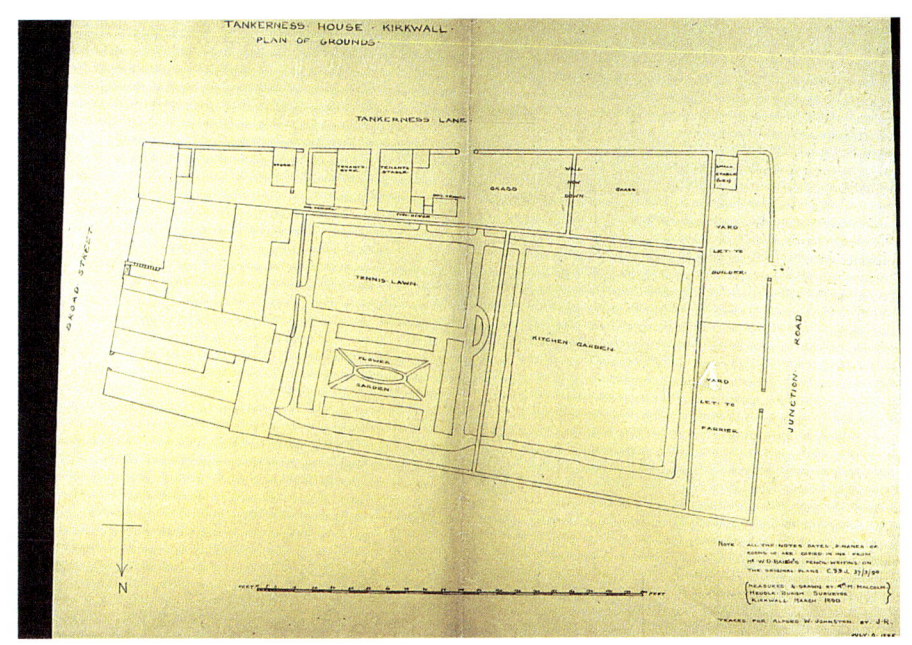

Plan of grounds, Tankerness House, in 1890.

Baikie family view Queen Victoria's Diamond Jubilee procession from the balcony in 1887. *T. Kent.*

Tankerness House garden in 2002.

*Profit Not Loss* 47

Tankerness House garden in 1898, Country Life Illustrated.

While the kitchen garden remained an important feature, by 1890 it shared the yard with a tennis lawn and a flower garden which was featured in the 16 December 1898 issue of Country Life Illustrated. '...*we discovered a charming garden in Kirkwall... the garden of Mr W. D. Baikie, of Tankerness House...Mr Baikie writes: "I have flowers for the table from the open air all the year round...except on rare occasions when the ground has been covered with snow."*'

Dover Baikie did not live to see the article in print, having died on 29th November of that year at the early age of 48. His brother, Alfred Cowan or Baikie, a consulting engineer who had spent much of his working life abroad, now succeeded to the estate.

A lock of the hair of 'Alfred the Little', 19 September 1864.

Alfred Cowan (later Baikie) front, 2nd right, in Mr Thomson's class in Kirkwall, early 1870s.

# Profit Not Loss

Alfred Baikie and his second wife Mary Anne Traill of Holland.

Alfred's first wife, Annie Traill Fotheringhame of Lynnfield (the sister of Mrs W. D. Baikie) with whom he had a son, Robert, had died in 1896, but in 1902 he remarried, this time with Mary Anne (Milanne) Stewart Traill, daughter of Thomas Traill of Holland in Papa Westray. He set about improving the Hall of Tankerness. He had the *"iron diningroom"* clad in stone, adding an upper floor, with the Baikie coat-of-arms and the motto 'Commodum non Damnum', which translates as 'Profit, not Loss', carved in stone. A skilled craftsman, he himself made the windows and wood panelling, and plastered the walls.

As 11th laird Alfred owned an estate which after the 1st World War was no longer profitable. The tenants still came to pay their annual rent at Tankerness House (where they were treated to a glass of ginger wine by the housekeeper Mrs Turfus), but Alfred began to break up the estate and one by one they bought their farms. The Baikies maintained a small flat in Tankerness House, much of which by the 1930s was divided and rented out.

Hall of Tankerness, August 1912, by Yeend King.

Alfred Baikie's replacement for 'the iron diningroom'.

Alfred Baikie's yacht *Nocti Luca*, c.1930.

Maraget Baikie's sailing dinghy *Cumpar* - Davy at the helm.

Hall of Tankerness in 1951, by Stanley Cursiter.

Lord Lieutenant and Mrs Alfred Baikie dressed to attend the coronation of King George VI and Queen Elizabeth.

*Profit Not Loss* 53

A popular figure, Alfred served as Lord Lieutenant for Orkney and Shetland from 1930 until his death in 1947. In 1938 he led the recruiting drive for the new 226th Heavy Anti-Aircraft Battery, a name which would become famous in Orkney's wartime service. He and his daughter Margaret were enthusiastic members of the Kirkwall amateur orchestra, Alfred playing the 'cello and Margaret the drums.

Margaret Baikie, 'Queen of the Nursery', by A. M. Traill.

Through both her father Alfred and her mother Mary, Margaret was descended from Robert Stewart Earl of Orkney, illegitimate son of King James V of Scotland and half-brother of Mary Queen of Scots. Margaret (Ming, as she was known to family and friends) served as a W.R.N.S. officer at *HMS Pyramus*, the naval headquarters at the Kirkwall Hotel, and later at *HMS Sparrowhawk*, the Royal Naval Air Station at Hatston, during the 2nd World War - the only W.R.N.S. officer to serve wholly in Orkney. After the death of her mother in October 1950 she married Harry Boden, an engineering officer with the Fleet Air Arm, and left Orkney to live in Cornwall, never to return. After her death in 1993, at her own request her ashes were scattered in the family burial ground at the Hall of Tankerness.

Margaret Baikie c. 1912, by Robert Gallon.

Margaret Baikie by Stanley Cursiter, 1947.

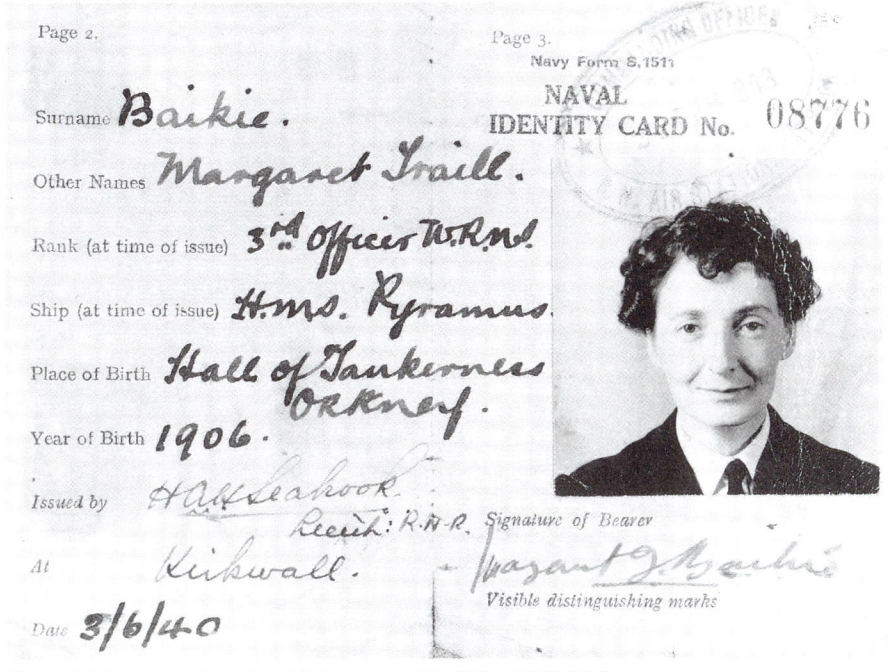

Naval Identity Card of Margaret Baikie W.R.N.S.

Calendar painted for Margaret Baikie by Marjorie Linklater.

Robert Baikie.

The last heir, Margaret's half-brother Robert, attended Loretto School in Musselburgh and Cambridge University where he graduated Master of Arts. He rowed for Clare College, was a fine shot and a promising cricketer, but a sporting injury resulting in a shortened leg prevented him joining the Royal Navy and denied him any overseas military service. He was commissioned into the Royal Garrison Artillery for his First World War service in Scapa Flow and Wales. He subsequently emigrated to Rhodesia and on the death of his stepmother returned as the 12th and last laird of Tankerness to completed the sale of the estate.

Alfred Baikie, Robert Baikie and Robert's daughter Jean , at the Hall of Tankerness.

Robert Baikie in the uniform of the Royal
Garrison Artillery, 1st World War.

Robert Baikie and his wife Ethel 'Biddy' Smith, whose mother was a
Traill of Holland in Papa Westray.

Profit Not Loss

The Hall of Tankerness with the home farm was sold to the Kirkwall accountant Bertie Bain, and remains the private residence of that family. Tankerness House was bought by Kirkwall Town Council in 1951 (the kitchen and mews had already been sold to the painter and decorator George Bain, and have since been built over). The house and shops continued to be let to tenants, but were now in a poor state.

Tankerness House before and after restoration.

For many years the establishment of a museum illustrating Orkney life, based on the collections of the defunct museum of the Orkney Antiquarian Society, had been discussed. Thanks to the efforts of the county librarian Evan MacGillivray, Dr Stanley Cursiter, Provost James Flett and others, a call for the demolition of the now crumbling Tankerness House was averted in favour of restoration, initially to house a museum in the south wing and new council chambers and committee rooms in the north wing. Grants from the Pilgrim Trust and the Historic Buildings Council for Scotland made possible a major restoration of the building which was carried out by an Edinburgh firm of architects, Ian G. Lindsay and Partners, winning a Civic Trust award.

Tankerness House after restoration, 1968.

*Profit Not Loss*

Under the Museums Association and the Carnegie United Kingdom Trust, Trevor Walden, Director of Leicester Museums & Art Gallery, was appointed to submit a report on the museum project. His recommendation that the whole building be used as a museum was accepted. He secured a grant for a lecturer and a team of students from the Department of Museum Studies at Leicester University to work with the honorary curator Evan MacGillivray in setting up the displays. Tankerness House Museum was opened by R. B. K. Stevenson, Keeper of the National Museum of Antiquities of Scotland, on Friday 31st May, 1968.

The Baikie Drawing Room, Tankerness House.

The Baikie Library.

Margaret Boden, pleased at the fate of the old house, bequeathed to the museum her paintings and furnishings. She wrote to Evan MacGillivray; *"It has always opened hospitable doors, and now is happily open to all".* She recalled life in the house as a child; *"Have you slidden down the bannisters? The brave and able began at the top of the house and, having carefully opened the front door, landed in the courtyard.*

*And there were those in my day who fired Verey lights out through the gate from the cannon. It is my dearest childhood recollection of the Old House.*

*Do you see that the steps at the very bottom of the garden are preserved. From them Janet Douglas escaped when chased by Red Coats for being a follower of Prince Charles Edward...The Peerie Sea came up to the wall then."* [ The family tradition has inverted the facts. Janet Douglas and her husband James Baikie, both staunch supporters of the Hanoverian king, were fleeing to Shetland from an incursion of Jacobite Highlanders which took place on 1st April 1746.]

Profit Not Loss

Tankerness House from the Kirk Green, 2002.

The courtyard, looking to the west wing.

The courtyard, with Dole Seat on the right.

The last laird's daughter Jean Clarke visited the house after the 2nd World War; *"I...recollect the powder room (for powdering wigs). My father always maintained that Tankerness House was haunted and that he personally had heard the ghost and rattling chains, and found one door opening the wrong way!"*

Since the reorganisation of local government in 1974 Tankerness House has belonged to Orkney Islands Council. The original Tankerness House Museum has grown and is now The Orkney Museum - the professionally staffed principal museum of Orkney life. Here visitors can acquire a vivid introduction to the pre-history and history of Orkney before visiting the many archaeological sites, specialist museums and heritage centres throughout the islands.

Two rooms of the museum are devoted to the Baikie family - the 1820 Baikie Drawing Room with family paintings and furniture, and the Baikie Library, with Robert the 7th laird's unique collection of books. In the 1820 stairwell are more family paintings and displays of memorabilia.

*Profit Not Loss*

It is remembered that the great copper ale brewing kettle listed by Janet Douglas in 1764 was still used by William Cowan Snr. in the ingleneuk fireplace of the brew house (now the Neolithic/ Bronze Age gallery of the Orkney Museum), early in the 20th century.

Baikie family punch bowl.

The old panelled *"Dining Roome"* of the south wing is now part of the Iron Age gallery. It is not hard to imagine a convivial company on a winter's night two centuries ago, puffing their clay pipes and passing the punch around the great mahogany table with its silver and pewter and delftware: and the flickering lights of the candelabra, suspended from the cupola above the table, reflecting in the gilded mirrors with the glow from the peat fire.

The descendants of the Baikies of Tankerness have maintained their interest in the old house. In June 2002 Jean Clarke and her daughter Gillian visited Orkney from their home in New Zealand. Jean Clarke commented: *"I think Tankerness House is absolutely beautiful now. There has been a tremendous restoration of the building and it has been very tastefully done."* They brought with them the portrait of their ancestor Murdoch Mackenzie, Orkney's last Church of Scotland bishop (1676-1688). The painting is now on long term loan to the Orkney Museum.

Jean Traill Clarke with her daughter Gillian Molony in Tankerness House, May 2002. *B. Wilson.*

Murdoch Mackenzie, last Church of Scotland Bishop of Orkney.

# DYNASTIC MARRIAGES, SCHOLARSHIP & ADVENTURE

The merchant lairds considered it essential to take a wife of their own class or above it, with all the social, political and pecuniary advantages that might ensue. George Baikie the 4th laird of Tankerness was married to Jean Stewart, granddaughter of the Earl of Sutherland. When James the 6th laird married Janet Douglas of the family of the Earl of Morton, she brought as her dowry the island of Egilsay.

With the estate inherited by the eldest son, siblings had to make their own way in the world. Again it was important to 'marry well'. This was the only hope for daughters to leave the family home, whether cementing blood ties with a neighbouring estate, or helping a favoured clergyman consolidate his social standing. James Baikie's daughter Anna in 1682 married George Traill of Quendale, who built a fine house for her in Kirkwall's Laverock (now Victoria Street).

For younger sons, university degrees, professions and careers in the army or navy were also an option. The 1st laird James Baikie's illegitimate son Thomas became minister of Rousay and Egilsay. Another Thomas Baikie, grand-nephew of James, was inducted as minister of St Magnus Cathedral in 1697, and this tale survives to illustrate kirk life of the period.

Thomas Baikie was appointed to replace the Reverend John Wilson who had been removed from office for continuing to support episcopacy - rule by bishops - abolished by the Church of Scotland in1688. John Wilson did not retire without a fight. He claimed the right to share the congregation with Thomas Baikie, and while he was prohibited from entering the cathedral, the illegal episcopal services which he held at his house in Anchor Close were tolerated by secretly sympathetic magistrates.

Thomas Baikie and his wife Elizabeth Fea of Whitehall in Stronsay lived in the former Catholic Church Treasury which stood in Broad Street opposite the cathedral. On Sunday 3rd January 1703, Mr Baikie was confined to bed through illness and there was no preacher available to give the sermon. John Wilson saw his chance and took it. With the compliance of a sympathetic beadle, David Seator, he caused the bells to be rung for morning service. On hearing this and observing from her window the gathering congregation, Mrs Baikie smelt a rat. She hauled her sick husband out of bed, threw a coat over his nightshirt and led him, still wearing his night-cap, into the cathedral. Between them the Baikies dragged John Wilson from the pulpit, dismissed the congregation and locked the cathedral door. David Seator lost his job.

James Baikie's son William qualified as Master of Arts. When William died in 1683 his library of 160 volumes he bequeathed to *"the Ministers of Kirkwall for a Publick Library to be kept within the Toune".* The 'Bibliotheck of Kirkwall' was housed in St Magnus Cathedral - the oldest public library in Scotland and forerunner of the Orkney County Library.

Straw work toilet box made by a French prisoner in the Napoleonic Wars.

*Profit Not Loss* 69

Two sons of Robert Baikie the 7th laird served in the navy. William travelled throughout the South Isles and Mainland of Orkney in 1795 drumming up support and attracting twenty recruits for the *Glory*, the new command of Captain (later Admiral) Graeme of Graemeshall. On 17th February 1813 while on *H.M.S. Royal George* at Port Mahon William wrote to his father of his brother James: *"...he is endeavouring to get me in a frigate. I hope his endeavours will prove successful as there is nothing to be learned here either in professional duty or in Navigation as there is no schoolmaster in the ship and many frigates have them..."*.

Robert's son Thomas was drowned on naval service in the Baltic in 1811.

Wine bottle of Captain John Baikie R. N.

Captain John Baikie R. N., drawn by Florence Sutherland-Graeme.

Naval uniform of Captain John Baikie.

Captain John Baikie, grand-nephew of the 6th laird, also served in the navy during the Napoleonic Wars. He then returned to Orkney to be the agent of the first bank in Kirkwall, a post which he held for 50 years. Sophia Cracroft, visiting his house in Kirkwall (now the Royal Bank of Scotland, across the lane from Tankerness House) with Lady Franklin in 1849, recorded in her diary: *"We had rather a pleasant evening - the old man Mr. John Baikie is very intelligent. Mrs Baikie, more sharp I should think than sweet. We looked over a Portfolio of good Prints which had been won as a prize in some lottery by Mr. Baikie. We had also music, I being the sole performer, but the room is exceedingly well adapted for singing...The evening concluded with supper at which we ate some of the very best and finest strawberries I have tasted any where."*

Almost a century later, Captain Baikie's great grand-daughter would marry Sir John Franklin's grand-nephew - but that is another story.

Captain John Baikie R. N.

Samuel Baikie, Master Builder.

Profit Not Loss

Captain Baikie's sons epitomised the Victorian spirit of enterprise. Samuel became a master builder, introducing in Kirkwall and Stromness Orkney's first steam-powered saw mills. Among other major projects he built Kirkwall Town Hall, and as a private speculation the terraced houses which grace East Road and Dundas Crescent.

Dundas Crescent terraced houses by Samuel Baikie. *T. Kent.*

Terraced houses by Samuel Baikie in East Road, Kirkwall. *T. Kent.*

Samuel's brother, Dr William Balfour Baikie, studied medicine in Edinburgh under a fellow islander, Professor Thomas Stewart Traill. As a student he was a founder member of the Orkney Antiquarian and Natural History Society, and during his holidays he made many expeditions to record flora and fauna with his school friend, Robert Heddle (later of Cletts and Melsetter). The resulting 'Natural History of Orkney - Part I (Zoology)', for nearly 50 years the only work of its kind, was published in 1848.

Dr. William Balfour Baikie.

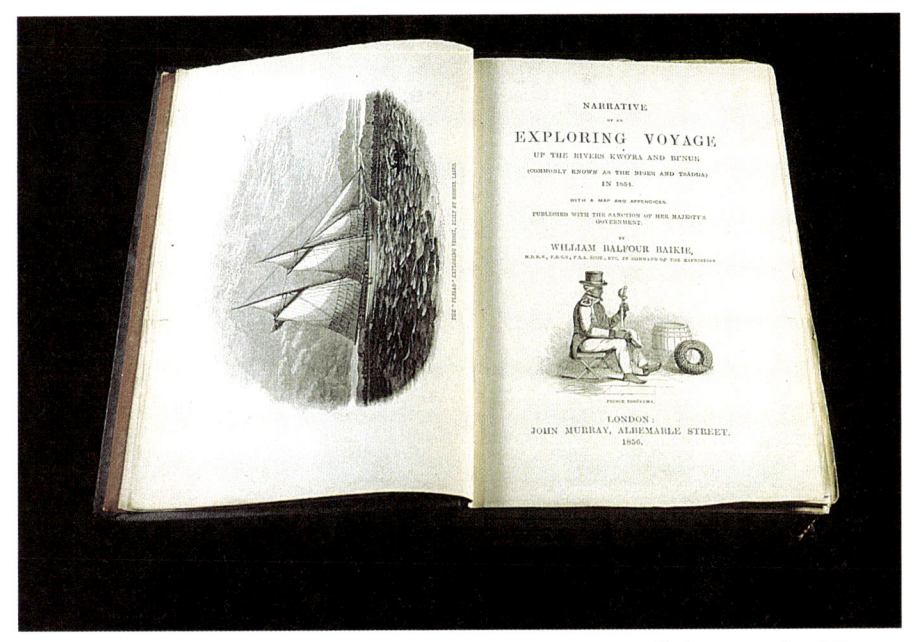

William Balfour Baikie's account of the 1854 expedition on the Niger.


On qualifying in medicine he became an assistant surgeon in the navy. Then in 1854 he sailed as surgeon and naturalist on an expedition to the River Niger to promote trade with the native peoples, taking over command when the leader died. Earlier explorers of the river, Mungo Park and Alexander Laing, had been killed, and many expedition members had died of malaria. On this river voyage on board the vessel *Pleiad* Baikie famously demonstrated the use of quinine as a prophylactic in removing the threat of the often fatal malaria virus, making possible the use of the Niger as a route to the interior of Africa. He persuaded the Government to promote annual steamer voyages to the river's trading posts. When the French novelist Jules Verne's adventurers set out on *Five Weeks in a Balloon* across Africa, among their charts was "Dr Baikie's Delta of the Niger".

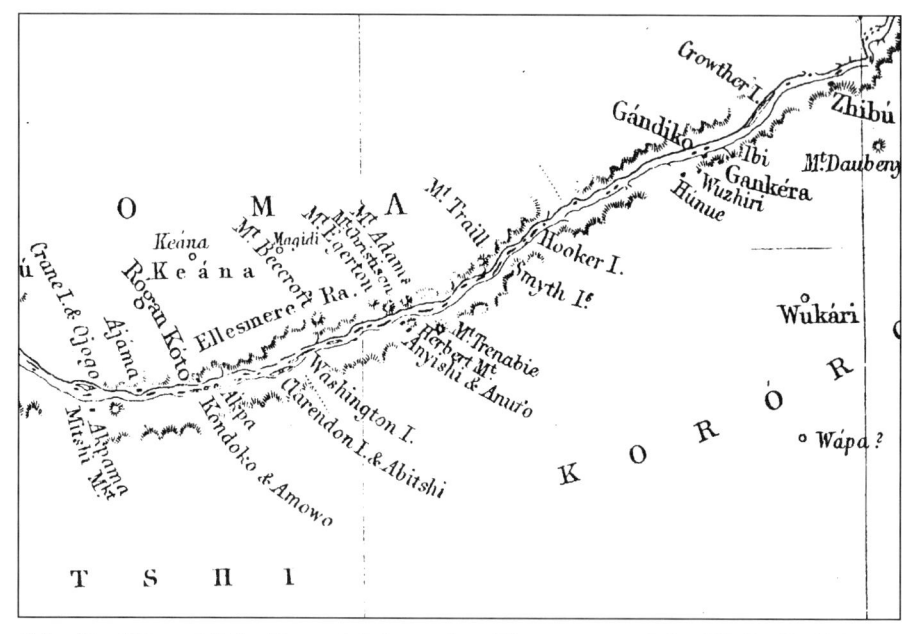

'Mt. Traill' and 'Mt. Trenabie' on the Niger, named by W. B. Baikie.

The Government recognised Baikie's worth by returning him as consul to the area in 1857. Because of his opposition to the slave trade on which the economy of the area still depended he was ill-received by some tribal chiefs, but gaining the trust of the powerful Emir of Nupe, ruler of the area, he founded and successfully ran the trading settlement of Lokoja at the confluence of the Niger and Benue rivers. By 1863 Lokoja was populated by two hundred natives, either refugees from slavery or slaves bought by Baikie in order to set them free. The Emir, noting Baikie's peace-keeping attributes, asked him to help govern his loose-knit states, and so he became the first of many thousands of British civil servants to govern what would become known as Nigeria.

Baikie 'went native' with enthusiasm, living in a mud hut, taking a mistress and fathering several Orcadian-African offspring. Garbed in sandals and the colourful local 'tobe' robe he became known as 'the King of Lokoja', dispensing law, medicine, education and religion in equal measure, but still having time to collect the vocabularies of many local languages, and to translate parts of the Bible into Hausa.

*Profit Not Loss* 77

Sieve and slave irons collected by Dr W. B. Baikie in Nigeria, and part of his extensive shell collection. *Stromness Museum.*

Such was the respect for William Baikie that his influence endures. To this day the word in the Ibo language for white man is *beke*, and *beke* is the suffix which identifies things introduced by him; thus *ewi-beke* (rabbit), *akwukwo-beke* (book), *manya-beke* (bottled drinks), *ala-beke* (Baikie's country, meaning Britain!).

On the way home in 1864 he died of dysentery in Freetown, Sierra Leone at the age of 39. Queen Victoria personally wrote to inform the Emir of Nupe of his death, reminding him of Baikie's opposition to the slave trade: *"We ask your Highness to use your great influence to stop this traffic, and to prevent the wars that are undertaken in many cases for the sole purpose of procuring slaves to be sold for shipment overseas...We request you to accept our best wishes and so we recommend you to the protection of the Almighty. Given at our Court at Osborne the 20th July, 1865, in the 29th year of our reign. Your good friend, Victoria."*

Dr William Balfour Baikie is commemorated by a monument which stands opposite that erected for the Arctic explorer, Dr John Rae, in St Magnus Cathedral.

By a happy coincidence, the African explorer's grand-niece Grace Rendall Baikie of Franklin Road in Stromness married in 1946 Major John Arthur Charles Franklin R. A., grand-nephew of the Arctic explorer Sir John Franklin.

Dr. William Balfour Baikie's monument in St Magnus Cathedral.

Grace Baikie and John Franklin on their wedding day.

# SOURCES

**Published**

1. Anderson, P./Black Patie (John Donald)
2. Anon/ A Garden in Orkney, Country Life Illustrated, Vol IV - No 102, Saturday December 17th 1898
3. Armstrong, K.A./ The Baikie Library at Tankerness House Museum, Kirkwall, Orkney, Library Review, Vol 40, No 1, 1991
4. Burgher, L./ Orkney, an Illustrated Architectural Guide (Royal Incorporation of Architects in Scotland 1981)
5. Fereday, R.P./ Orkney Feuds and the '45 (Kirkwall Grammar School 1980)
6. Fereday, R.P./The Orkney Balfours 1747-99 (Tempus Reparatum 1990)
7. Fereday, R.P./The Autobiography of Samuel Laing of Papdale 1780-1868 (Bellavista Publications 2000)
8. Fyfe, C./Introduction to the 1987 reprint of Natural History of Orkney. Part I. W.B. Baikie, M.D., and Robert Heddle
9. Goodfellow, A./ Dr Robert Paterson of Orkney (Goodfellow 1920)
10. Gramont, S. de / The Strong Brown God - The Story of the Niger River (Hart Davis, MacGibbon, London 1975)
11. Hossack, B.H./ Kirkwall in the Orkneys (William Peace & Son 1900)
12. Hewison, W.S./ Who Was Who in Orkney (Bellavista Publications 1998)
13. Mackintosh, W.R./ Curious Incidents from the Ancient Records of Kirkwall (Orcadian Office 1892)
14. Marwick, E.W./ William Balfour Baikie, Explorer of the Niger (Kirkwall, 1965)
15. Marwick, H./ The Baikies of Tankerness, Vol 4 Orkney Miscellany (Kirkwall 1957)
16. McGavin, N.A./ Excavations in Kirkwall 1978 (P.S.A.S. 1982)
17. New Statistical Account of Scotland, 1841 (Blackwood and Sons 1842)
18. Scott, Sir W./ Notes to *The Pirate*.
19. Shaw, F.J./ The Northern and Western Islands of Scotland (John Donald 1980)
20. Statistical Account of Scotland, 1795-1798
21. Stott, L./ Robert Louis Stevenson and the Highlands and Islands of Scotland (Creag Darach Publications, Stirling 1992)
22. Thomson, W.P.L./ The New History of Orkney (Merkat Press, Edinburgh 1987, 2001)
23. Wenham, S./ A More Enterprising Spirit - the Parish and People of Holm in 18th Century Orkney (Bellavista Publications 2001)

**Unpublished**

24. The Baikie Papers, Orkney Library Archives
25. Diary of Sophia Cracroft, The Scott Polar Research Institute, University of Cambridge
26. Boden, Margaret/ correspondence, The Baikie Papers, Orkney Library Archives
27. Clarke, Jean Traill/ correspondence, The Baikie Papers, Orkney Library Archives
28. Holtom, Christopher/ correspondence re the Minervian Library
29. Bain, Lann/ private correspondence